IMAGINE THAT—
A CHILD'S GUIDE TO YOGA

Written by Kenneth K. Cohen
Illustrated by Joan Hyme

SANTA BARBARA BOOKS
SANTA BARBARA, CALIFORNIA

ISBN 0-915520-55-9

Typeset by Jim Cook
Santa Barbara

Printed by Permanent Typesetting & Printing Co., Ltd.
Hong Kong

To our beloved Papa, His Holiness
Reverend Sri Swami Satchidananda,
a Father of Divine Wisdom and Love,
a child of Eternal Peace and Joy.

May this book serve as a tiny seed
to be planted by a loving grown-up
into the heart of a small child.

Contents

Imagine that you are a boat,
 a bird, a bow, a tree.
Imagine that you are the things
 that you'd most like to be.
Then be like them, pretend you are,
 be just like what you see!

Introduction

Once upon a time, a yoga instructor asked himself this question: How can I share that which is ancient (yoga) with that which is new (a child)? One day, as he sat reflecting in the posture of meditation, the answer came: "build a bridge." And so he did.

Imagine That—A Child's Guide to Yoga is a book of illustrated poetry and a complete instruction guide for a child's study of Hatha Yoga. The intention of each poem and illustration is to fill young minds with a sense of inner harmony and with the inspiration of nature.

Yoga is an age-old science, dedicated to the health of the body and to peace, strength and clarity of mind. Good digestion, sound sleep, vitality and enthusiasm, proper functioning of the internal organs, flexibility and muscle tone, happiness and continuous ease are some of the benefits to be achieved through the regular practice of yoga.

Health and peace is the birthright of every child. It is our loving duty as parents and educators to provide the young with a knowledge of how to maintain and develop these two most precious gifts.

May all be happy, may all be free from disabilities, may all look to the good of others, may none suffer from sorrow.

—An ancient Yogic Prayer

Guidelines for Parents and Educators

Hatha Yoga is a comprehensive system of gentle, non-stress postures, stretches, balancing positions, breathing, relaxation and meditation practices. A regular discipline provides us with the opportunity to experience agility, vitality, and clarity of awareness in our daily lives. The quality of what we are to become is often guided by what we have been educated to be, thus the contribution of *Imagine That—A Child's Guide to Yoga*, a book to held the young ones alone.

SUGGESTIONS AND HINTS

1. First and foremost, be creative and real in your sharing. That is a language children understand best. Practice yoga regularly yourself; then insight and inspiration will flow easily through you.

2. All children have varying attention spans and levels of flexibility. Gear your instructions accordingly. A session's duration should be directly correlated to a child's age and interest.

3. Younger children seem to take to yoga most readily within the context of play, whereas older children seem to appreciate more adult explanations in terms of basic philosophy and benefits to the body.

4. The postures (asanas) should be done on an empty stomach, either before meals or at least two hours after a meal. A light beverage up to half an hour before yoga is okay.

5. With regard to food, study principles of healthy diet and nutrition, then incorporate your understanding into nourishing meals made with plenty of love.

6. The suggested time for each pose can vary somewhat according to the child's ability. Observe carefully that no tremor or strain is taking place. Never keep a child in a posture longer than the maximum duration prescribed, as the pose may become counter-productive by putting undue pressure on a particular system of the body.

7. The headstand and other difficult poses should not be practiced until a child is at least twelve years old.

8. Normal breathing accompanies all postures and at no point should the breath be held unnecessarily.

9. Overextension in stretching or bouncing and fidgeting should be watched for and corrected. An asana is any pose that the body can assume with steadiness and ease.

10. Short rests complement the beneficial effects of the postures. Again, depending on the child's age and attention span, you may find it useful to save a rest period until after several postures.

11. Wear loose-fitting clothing for yoga, and see that the floor or

ground on which the asanas are to be practiced is level and comfortable to the body.

The Hatha Yoga asanas taught in *Imagine That—A Child's Guide to Yoga* relfect the traditional foundation from which literally thousands of postures and their variations have evolved. As a child becomes more adept at any of the given practices, new postures and variations of the basic sequence may be added.

REST SECTION

The guided relaxation truly complements the completion of the Hatha postures. This practice, call *Yoga Nidra* in Sanskrit, releases any remaining tensions and stresses from the body and restores vitality to all of the interal systems. This practice can last anywhere from three to ten minutes.

BREATHING SECTION

To breath deeply is to live fully. The study and practice of breathing helps to increase the oxygen capacity of the lungs and the energy of the body and mind. Technically the practice of breathing *(pranayama)* is a process for learning to explore and experience the subtle currents of energy that permeate the body/mind and all of nature. The practice of proper breathing can help a child develop concentration and a calm, clear and strong mind. Once the child moves beyond an initial restlessness and aversion to being still, he or she will experience the benefits of breathing, and thereafter seek this practice more and more.

MEDITATION SECTION

When a child's mind is fully alert and has a serene quality, then the experience of deep inner peace, joy and understanding can unfold. This is meditation. The guided meditation section called Inner Space is a creative attempt to shift the normal focus of a child's attention from the activities of the external world to the peace and clarity within.

Dance to the Sun

Soorya Namaskaram

These are the twelve positions in each round of the Dance to the Sun.

Making the Body Ready: Stand up tall with your legs together and arms at your sides.

Now to Begin:

Position 1: Palms together, fingertips to lips.

Position 2: Locking your thumbs, stretch your arms high overhead along side your ears. Look up.

Position 3: Bend forward, keeping your knees straight. Look at your knees.

Position 4: Stretch your left leg back with your left knee on the ground. Place your fingertips in line with your toes (right foot remains between your hands). Lean slightly forward and look up.

Position 5: Move right foot back to meet your left foot, buttocks high up in the air, head between your arms. Heels of your feet are pressing gently to the ground.

Position 6: Your knees, chest and chin, in that order, come to the ground. Your pelvic area is kept a few inches off the floor. Your fingertips are in line with your shoulders, arms are in close to your ribcage and your elbows point upward.

Position 7: Lower your pelvis to the ground as your upper body slides forward. Slowly raise your head, then your chest off the ground. Try to rely on the strength of your back muscles, using your hands mainly for supporting the weight of your body.

Position 8: Raise your body back into Position 5.

Position 9: Try to bring your left foot up between your arms. Your right knee comes to the ground. Lean slightly forward and look up.

Position 10: Move your right foot forward to meet the left. Keep your knees straight as in Position 3.

Position 11:   Stretch your arms high overhead, locking your thumbs as in Position 2.

Position 12:   Place your palms together, fingertips to lips as in Position 1.

Rest: Bring your arms alongside your body, and your legs shoulder-width apart. Close your eyes to rest.

Suggestions: First, hold each position separately. Afterward, allow each position to flow slowly and smoothly into the next like a graceful dance. Do not overexert your body by stretching too far or moving too rapidly.

Time: Repeat two or three times each yoga session.

Benefits: The Dance to the Sun adds flexibility to the spine and tones muscles. It's a general tonic for all systems of the body and helps develop a prayerful attitude of the mind.

Early when the morning sun
Sits up on the horizon
Yogi children greet the day
In a very special way.

Golden Friend, I learned a dance
So I could let you know
How happy I am every day
You come to say hello.

4. Yet with each morning you look so bright and young

5. All the birds sing their songs to you

6. The animals in the fields play merrily through your day

10. In the dance called Growing Up and Growing Old

11. Like a baby seed growing to become a Wise Old Tree

12. Roots reaching deep into the Earth,
branches raising upward toward the sky

The Cobra

Bhujangasana

Making the Body Ready: Lie down on your stomach. Relax your body. Place your palms on the ground beneath your shoulders. Bring your legs together; point your toes and place your forehead on the ground. Keep your arms close to your ribcage and your elbows pointing upward.

Now to Begin: Raise your head slowly upward (hold for five seconds). Then raise your chest slightly off the floor without putting pressure on your palms (hold for five seconds). Now gently push against the floor with your palms to develop the backward arch (hold for five seconds).

Rest: Slowly lower your chest and forehead to the ground. Bring your cheek to the side. Place your arms down alongside of your body and your legs apart. Close your eyes to rest.

Time: Repeat once or twice. Hold the pose from fifteen to thirty seconds each time. You may arch up completely without pausing once mastery and ease are achieved.

Suggestions: Do not jerk your body upward. Try to mostly rely on your back muscles, using your arms primarily for support.

Variation: An advanced variation is to straighten your arms and bend your knees so your toes are pointing straight toward your head.

Benefits: The Cobra strengthens the upper back and vertebrae of the spine. It expands the chest cage, thereby increasing the capacity of the lungs.

Hooded Cobra on the ground,
Won't you raise your diamond crown
High into a morning breeze
That blows so sweetly through the
trees

The Grasshopper
Salabasana

Making the Body Ready: Lie down on your stomach, with your legs together. Slide your hands under your thighs, palms facing upward. Now slide your elbows under your stomach and bring your chin to the ground.

Now to Begin: Stretch your right leg and point your toes. Slowly raise your right leg off the ground, keeping your knee straight. Try to keep your body from tilting to one side. Slowly lower your right leg. Do the same movement with your left leg.

Rest: Bring your cheek to the side. Slide your arms out from under your body, spreading your legs apart. Close your eyes and quietly rest for a while.

Time: Hold each leg up from ten to twenty seconds. Repeat twice.

Suggestions: Do not lift your legs up too high or your body will tilt to one side.

Variations: Older children may try to raise both legs simultaneously and hold from five seconds to fifteen seconds. When first beginning to raise both legs together, only raise them a little. When your back muscles become stronger you can try to raise them higher and hold the pose longer.

Benefits: The Grasshopper strengthens the lower back and vertebrae of the spine. It also strengthens and tones the lower abdomen.

Green Grasshopper runs around,
Always hopping up and down.
On your flower look and see,
Can you be as still as me?

The Bow

Dhanurasana

Making the Body Ready: Bend your knees and grab hold of your ankles. Bring your forehead to the ground. Keep your arms straight without bending your elbows. Keep your body relaxed.

Now to Begin: Slowly and easily, lift your thighs a little way off the ground. Keep your shoulders relaxed. Now begin to raise your head and lift your chest off the floor. Your stomach should be the only part of you that is on the ground. Hold still from ten seconds to thirty seconds and then slowly come down.

Rest: Release your ankles and allow your legs to return to the ground. Bring your legs apart with your arms close to your body and your cheek to the side. Close your eyes and quietly rest for a little while.

Time: Repeat once or twice. Hold each pose from ten seconds to thirty seconds.

Suggestions: Do not raise your legs and chest too quickly. Always move very slowly in and out of the Bow pose. Never bend your elbows while lifting your legs. Do not raise your legs so high that you feel uncomfortable.

Benefits: The Bow pose strengthens and tones the stomach. It also aids in digestion and elimination. It combines the benefits of the Cobra and Grasshopper poses.

I will be an Archer
My body is the Bow.
I use my arms as bowstrings
To draw back my arrow.

The Folding Leaf

Pashimothanasana

Making the Body Ready: Lie on your back and bring your legs together. Stretch your arms overhead next to your ears. Sit up and stretch your arms toward the sky. Hold this position from five to ten seconds.

Now to Begin: Very slowly lean forward. Try to develop your bend from the hip rather than from the waist as you reach toward your knees. If this is easy, then reach for your ankles or even your toes. Keep your elbows slightly bent and the backs of your knees on the ground.

Rest: Return to a sitting position and lower your back to the ground. Bring your arms alongside your body with your palms facing upward and your legs apart. Close your eyes and rest for a while.

Time: Hold this pose from twenty seconds to one minute.

Suggestions: Remember to keep the backs of your knees on the ground and have your toes pointing upward to give an extra stretch to your legs. Do not overextend. Just allow your body to gently fold in half.

Variations: Keep your left leg stretched out, and either tuck the sole of your right foot into the side of your left thigh, or if comfortable, place the outside of your ankle on top of your thigh. Bend as far as you can comfortably and hold on to your extended leg from fifteen to thirty seconds. Repeat with your right leg. This is called the Half Folding Leaf. (*Janusirsasana*)

Benefits: The Folding Leaf tones and massages the inner organs of the abdomen and stretches the back muscles and the vertebrae of the spine. This pose also relieves tightness in the backs of the legs and stiffness of the lower back.

Like a Folding Leaf I'll close
To rest in forward bending pose
Then wait to catch a passing breeze
That carries me where it
may please.

The Candle

Sarvangasana

Making the Body Ready: Lie on your back. Bring your legs together and your arms close to your body with your palms pressed down on the ground.

Now to Begin: Putting pressure on your palms, bring your knees to your chest. Continue to roll your hips and chest upward until your legs, now straight, are over your head and parallel to the floor. Place your hands on the lower back to maintain your balance, then slowly raise your legs until they are perpendicular to the ground.

Rest: To come down from the Candle posture, bend your knees toward your chest. Bring your palms to the ground and lower your back, then your legs. After your legs touch the ground, spread them apart. Roll your head from side to side once or twice. Face your palms upward. Close your eyes and rest a little while.

Time: Hold the Candle once for thirty seconds and gradually build up to three minutes.

Suggestions: Do not jerk up into the Candle. An older child or parent can help guide your legs and body both up and down until you can do this posture by yourself, be still and breathe normally through your nose. It is better not to talk, laugh or swallow when in the Candle, as this may make your throat feel a bit sore.

Variations: Older children can try keeping their legs fully extended as they go up and come down out of the pose. After some time, when you can hold the posture easily for the prescribed length of time, you may carefully place one arm, then the other, on the front or sides of your thighs, resulting in an unsupported shoulder stand. The balance is on the back of your neck and shoulders for this more advanced variation.

Benefits: The Candle helps to tone a gland located in the throat called the thyroid. This gland is responsible for the general health of the entire body. The inverted posture brings a good supply of blood to the brain cells and oxygen to the upper lungs. It also relieves gravitational pressure from the legs and the internal organs of the body.

Like a Candle I will burn
To give the darkness light
In happiness and health I know
The world becomes so bright

The Fish

Matsyasana

Making the Body Ready: Lie flat on your back. Bring your legs together and hold the sides of your thighs.

Now to Begin: Use your elbows to lift your head and upper body. Arch gently backward, expanding your chest and touching the crown of your head to the ground. Bring your head in as close as possible to your buttocks to make a nice arch. Relax your shoulders and jaw by keeping a smile on your lips. Breath slowly and deeply through your nose.

Rest: To come out of the Fish pose, hold the sides of your thighs and, using your elbows to lift the upper body, inhale and sit up. As you exhale, lower your body to the floor. Roll your head a few times from side to side, shrug your shoulders gently and let your head find the center. Keep your arms close to your body, your palms facing upward, and your legs apart. Close your eyes and rest a little while.

Time: Repeat once or twice and hold each time from fifteen seconds to forty-five seconds.

Suggestions: Always follow the shoulder stand with the Fish pose as they complement one another in their effects on the body. To help the child maintain an arch and not strain while coming out of the Fish, an older child or parent can place a hand on the youngster's back between his shoulder blades as a support.

Variations: The Fish helps to increase the ability of the lungs to breathe in fresh air. It also helps to strengthen the back muscles and spine.

If you ask me what I wish,
I think I'd like to be a Fish
Swimming in a mountain stream.
What fun! This world is such a
dream.

The Tree

Vrikshasana

Making the Body Ready: This is a balancing posture, so stand up tall with your legs close together and your arms close to your body.

Now to Begin: Take hold of your left foot with both your hands and slowly raise your left leg upward by bending your left knee. Place the sole of your left foot on the side of your right thigh or at the top of your thigh (if you can do the Lotus posture), then slowly raise your arms into either of the three different positions that the boys and girls are doing on the facing page. Switch and do the same with your other leg.

Rest: Slowly lower your arms and legs and stand in a comfortable position.

Time: Hold the pose on each leg for fifteen to sixty seconds.

Suggestions: Try not to hop. Keep your eyes on a single fixed point to help you keep still. If you feel very confident that you are steady, then try to close your eyes and see if you can still keep your balance.

Benefits: This posture helps develop balance and coordination of the body.

I am like the tall Oak Tree
Firmly rooted in the ground.
Animals rest under me,
Where shade and shelter can be
found.

The Dancing King

Natarajasana

Making the Body Ready: This is also a balancing posture, so stand up tall with your legs close together and your arms alongside your body.

Now to Begin: Slowly bend your right leg backward. Catch hold of your right ankle. Extend your left arm toward the sky. Do the same posture with your other arm and leg.

Rest: Slowly lower your arm and release your ankle. Stand with your legs apart in a very relaxed way.

Time: Hold onto each leg from fifteen seconds to sixty seconds.

Suggestions: Try not to hop around or come up on your toes. See if you can remain absolutely still while in the Dancing King posture. If you look at a point in front of you, it will help you keep your body balanced. Breathe in a relaxed manner. If you are comfortable and steady, you may try to gently increase the arch of the posture by pulling your leg upward. Keep your elbow straight rather than bent. If you can hold the posture easily, close your eyes and see if you can still keep your balance. This is a little harder.

Benefits: This posture also helps develop balance and coordination of the body.

I will be a Dancing King
Who can do most anything.
Rooted in the Earth I'll try
To raise one leg
and touch the sky.

The Boat

Nauasana

Making the Body Ready: Lie down on your stomach. Bring your legs together and place your arms behind your back, holding your wrists or elbows, whichever is more comfortable. Place your chin on the ground.

Now to Begin: Raise your chin, chest and legs slowly off the ground so you are balancing on your stomach. Breathe normally through your nose.

Rest: Slowly come out of the pose. Release your arms. Bring your cheek to the side and draw your legs apart. Close your eyes and rest a little while.

Time: Do the Boat twice and hold it from ten to thirty seconds each time.

Suggestions: Do not jerk up or come down too quickly. Only go up as high as is comfortable so there is no strain on your body when the posture is held.

Variation: Stretch your arms overhead and lock your thumbs. Keep your arms next to your ears while moving into the pose. Look at your thumbs.

Benefits: The Boat strengthens the abdomen and the internal digestive organs.

Like a Boat upon the waves
We'll sail across the sea
Then ride the winds that brings us
      home
As swiftly as can be.

The Seashell

Yoga Mudra

Making the Body Ready: Sit up tall in a comfortable cross-legged meditation posture. (See the picture of the children on the next page and decide which cross-legged position is easiest for you.)

Now to Begin: Bring your arms behind your back and clasp your wrists. Slowly lean forward over your crossed legs as far as is comfortable without raising your buttocks off the ground. Close your eyes and allow your head, neck and shoulders to relax.

Time: Hold the Seashell from thirty to sixty seconds.

Suggestions: Remember not to allow your buttocks to leave the ground. Do not bounce your body to try to go further down. Your body weight alone will help loosen your muscles so that you can lower your head to the floor.

Benefits: The Seashell stretches the back and the spine, and increases their flexibility. This posture also improves the ability to digest food and eliminate waste materials from the body.

Like a tiny little seashell,
I rest upon the sand,
And listen to the ocean winds
Blowing o'er the land.

Lotus Flower
Padmasana

The Lotus Flower is the posture of meditation. When meditation is practiced, the mind becomes very clear, calm and strong. Then one blossoms with peace, understanding, and love. If you sit like the silent mountain every day, gradually you may come to feel a deep happiness inside. It is there within that silence that all of nature will become a beautiful symphony of music to you.

Making the Body Ready: In learning to sit comfortably in either the Half Lotus or Full Lotus posture, start with this warmup stretching exercise.

Bring your legs out in front of you. Bend your right leg into a cross-legged position. Take hold of your right foot and ankle and place them on top of your left thigh. With both hands, put a gentle pressure on the inside of your right knee. This exercise helps to stretch the inner thigh muscles. Hold this position from thirty to sixty seconds, then reverse legs.

Now to Begin: Sit up tall, without making your body feel stiff. Place your legs into one of the cross-legged positions like the children on the next page, with your hands resting either on your lap or knees.

Time: The Lotus Flower posture can be held anywhere from thirty seconds to sixty seconds at the end of the Hatha Yoga Asana series. This asana follows the Seashell and comes before the rest section. When the Lotus Flower is done during a child's meditation (rather than as a posture), it can be held anywhere from one minute to fifteen minutes or more, depending upon the child's interest and absorption in the daily practice. The two best times for meditation are the early morning right after cleansing and before breakfast, and in the evening before sleep.

Suggestions: The Half and Full Lotus leg positions can cause an unnecessary amount of strain to your knees if your leg muscles are not sufficiently supple. Therefore, in the beginning exercise care and caution. Once your leg muscles are loose these two postures help keep your body very steady for meditation. It may be helpful to sit on a cushion or pillow to keep your body straight and tall.

Benefits: The Lotus Flower posture, when practiced daily, brings many wonderful benefits to the mind and body. The entire nervous system is made strong and the energy of the body/mind is qualitatively increased.

See the section on Meditation for guided instructions.

The mighty mountain sits so still
And listens as a soft breeze blows
Its flower music to the hills
And by the lake where the Lotus grows.

A Child's Meditation On Rest

Imagine that you are resting on a white sandy beach. The sun is shining brightly overhead and a gentle breeze is blowing from the sea. The sea breeze touches the toes of your feet and makes them feel relaxed. The gentle breeze moves up your legs, then plays with your fingers and your arms. Your back feels as if it is slowly sinking into the sand. Imagine that the sun's shining rays are warming your stomach and your chest, your chin and your nose, eyelids and ears, forehead, and the crown of your head.

Imagine that it is a quiet day. The sky is clear blue, and if you listen very carefully, you can hear the sound of . . . (think of your own word) . . . around you. Listen closely and you can hear the sound of the air quietly passing in and out of your nose. Listen more closely and you might even be able to hear the thumpety-thump sound of your own heartbeat.

Because you are now so relaxed, you might even feel as if you were floating on a puffy white cloud. Imagine that, and let your happiness grow and shine like the sun over the giant mountains of the earth; over the green grass of the fields; over the blue waters of the sea. Let your happiness shine over all of the animals in the forest and over all of the people of the world. Be like the sun and let your happiness, health, and love shine.

I am like a blade of grass
Covering the land.
I am like a small seashell
Lying on the sand.

I am like a lily pad
Resting on the sea.
I am like a tiny bird
Sleeping in a tree.

I am like a small white cloud
Floating in the sky.
I am like a summer breeze
Gently passing by.

I am like the silver moon
Sailing cross the night.
I am like the golden sun
Shining with delight.

Breathing

We live in an invisible ocean called air. When the wind blows you can feel air playing against your skin. Air is energy for all life. As we breathe through the nose, air fills our lungs like it fills a balloon, then travels with the blood to every part of the body to become food for the tiny body cells. As we breathe out, all the old air goes back into the sky.

The Gentle Breath

Breathe slowly and gently through your nose and feel your abdomen and chest expand. Then empty the air very slowly out of your nose again and feel your chest and then your stomach relax. Can you sit up tall and still? Now imagine that a little candle is glowing at the very center of your heart. As the air goes inside your lungs, the candle grows bright, and as the air goes out, image that the world is being warmed with your light of happiness and love.

The Sun and Moon Breath

Continue to breathe deep and gently. Bring your right hand up to your nose and close off the side of your right nostril with your thumb. Exhale from and then inhale into the left nostril (moon). Place your fourth and pinky finger on your left nostril, release your thumb, and slowly let the air out, then in through your right nostril (sun). Do this very gently five to ten times. You will begin to feel very peaceful inside.

The Humming Bee Breath

Keep your eyes closed and slowly take in air through your nose, and as you breathe out, pretend that you are a humming bee and:

1. Make a long *high* humming sound
2. Make a long *low* humming sound
3. Make a long *loud* humming sound
4. Make a long *soft and sweet* humming sound
5. Now make no sound at all...but listen

Meditation
Inner Space

Everyone knows something about outer space. It is filled with people and planets, raindrops and oceans, trees and skies; just about anything that you can imagine. But do you know about inner space? Not very many people do. That is because inner space is not a place you can find on any map.

But if we close our eyes, sit real still, and then imagine that we are like a tall and mighty mountain that is listening to the song of a gentle wind, perhaps we will find a bright and beautiful world inside our hearts called inner space.

When you sit for meditation, keep your back, neck and head in a straight line without being stiff as a statue. Fold your hands in your lap or rest them on your knees...Be still. Can you stay like this for a minute or more?

Now imagine that a soft and beautiful ray of light is glowing right over your head, and as you breathe in, the light travels down into your heart. As you breathe out, the light travels up and shines once more above your head. Can you imagine that with each and every breath?

Inner Space is something like a flower that we water each day to help it grow. Every morning, take inside the invisible light of happiness above your head to help water the flower of your heart with love. Remember to do this for at least a minute or more. And at night, again sit quietly; this time imagine that your light is glowing like a shining star of peace above the world.

Inner Space

I feel so light and bright inside
A smile is on my face
A happy glow is in my heart
Yes, I'm in Inner Space!